Ana's Community Helpers

Shanya Worthy

ROSEN
COMMON CORE
READERS

Rosen
Classroom™

New York

Published in 2013 by The Rosen Publishing Group, Inc.
29 East 21st Street, New York, NY 10010

Book Design: Michael Harmon

Photo Credits: Cover CandyBox Images/Shutterstock.com; p. 5 Dmitriy Shoronosov/Shutterstock.com; p. 7 © iStockphoto.com/monkeybusinessimages; pp. 9, 11 wavebreakmedia ltd./Shutterstock.com; p. 13 Comstock/Comstock Images/Getty Images; p. 15 (male mail carrier) © iStockphoto.com/joshblake; p. 15 (female mail carrier) Paul Burns/Blend Images/Getty Images.

ISBN: 978-1-4488-8698-2
6-pack ISBN: 978-1-4488-8699-9

Manufactured in the United States of America

CPSIA Compliance Information: Batch #WS12RC: For further information contact Rosen Publishing, New York, New York at 1-800-237-9932.

Word Count: 21

Contents

Ana sees dentists.

Ana sees firefighters.

Ana sees doctors.

Ana sees librarians.

Ana sees truck drivers.

Ana sees mail carriers too.

Words to Know

dentists

doctors

firefighters

librarians

mail carriers

truck drivers

Index